The Photo Box

by Cameron Macintosh

illustrated by Katie Kear

OXFORD
UNIVERSITY PRESS
AUSTRALIA & NEW ZEALAND

"Good morning, everybody," said Mrs Gill to her pupils. "This is a special day. We are going to talk about the kind of work you would like to do when you are older."

"I want to work in my mum's fruit shop," said Charlotte.

"I want to be a musician!" said Zak.

"I want to be a nurse," said Ben.

None of the other children wanted to be nurses.

"Why would you want to do that?" asked Zak.

"I want to help people get better when they are hurt or sick," said Ben.

Zak shrugged.

"This weekend, I want you all to find out about the work you would like to do," said Mrs Gill. "Then you will talk to the class about it."

The next day, Ben and his mum went to see Gran, to help clean her house.

They were busy cleaning Gran's study when Mum asked Ben to take some boxes out.

As Ben took a box towards the door, he saw some photos inside. Some of the photos were in colour, but most were black and white.

"Look, Mum," he said. "Lots of old photos and a letter."

"We should show these to Gran," replied Mum.

A few minutes later, Mum and Ben brought the whole box of photos to the kitchen.

"Look, Gran," said Ben. "We found some photos of you, and a letter."

"That's not me in the photos," said Gran. "That is my mother when she was young."

"What's in this letter?" asked Ben.

"My mother's father did not want her to be a nurse," said Gran. "She wrote to him to try to change his mind."

Gran read the letter aloud.

"It's my dream to become a nurse," Gran read.
"I want to help people who have come home
from the war. I know I'm strong enough to do it.
It will be a good decision."

"Did she become a nurse?" asked Ben.

"Yes, she did," said Gran.

"That's incredible," said Ben. "I had no idea that your mum was a nurse. I'm so happy that her father did not cause her to give up on her dream."

"There are many photos of her at work," said Gran. "Look at this one."

Gran took out a photo of her mother standing next to an older nurse.

"That was the head nurse," said Gran. "Mother told me that she was usually very serious, but that she had a warm heart."

"How long was your mum a nurse?" asked Ben.

"She was a nurse for five years," said Gran. "She helped many people who had been hurt in the war to get better and start new lives back at home. She said it was a great honour."

Ben was impressed. "I want to be a nurse, too," he said.

"Nursing would suit you," said Gran in agreement.
"You are full of kindness, just like my mother."

"Would you mind if I showed your photos to my class?" asked Ben.

"Not at all, as long as you are careful," said Gran. "I would love the other kids to see them."

Back at school, Ben showed Gran's photos to the class. "My Gran's mum was a nurse," he said. "She helped many people get better after the war."

Everybody wanted to know all about her. Ben told them everything he knew.

After Ben's speech, Zak sat next to him. "I thought it was strange that you wanted to be a nurse," he said, "but now I understand."